FEMALE

Pop Di

MW00563064

Sing Along with 8 Great-Sounding Tracks

Contents

Alfred Publishing Co., Inc.
16320 Roscoe Blvd., Suite 100
P.O. Box 10003
Van Nuys, CA 91410-0003
alfred.com

ISBN-10: 0-7390-4441-9 (Book and CD)
ISBN-13: 978-0-7390-4441-4 (Book and CD)

Cover Art:
Microphone: © Georg Neumann GmbH, Berlin
Background: © istockphoto.com/Flashworks

Because of You

Words and Music by
KELLY CLARKSON, BEN MOODY and DAVID HODGES

Ooh, ooh, ooh.

Verse 1:
I will not make
the same mistakes that you did.
I will not let myself
cause my heart so much misery.
I will not break
the way you did, you fell so hard.
I've learned the hard way
to never let it get that far.

Chorus:
Because of you,
I never stray too far from the sidewalk.
Because of you,
I learned to play on the safe side so I don't get hurt.
Because of you,
I find it hard to trust not only me,
but ev'ryone around me.
Because of you, I am afraid.

Verse 2:
I lose my way,
and it's not too long before you point it out.
I cannot cry,
because I know that's weakness in your eyes.
I'm forced to fake a smile,
a laugh ev'ry day of my life.
My heart can't possibly break
when it wasn't even whole to start with.

Chorus:
Because of you,
I never stray too far from the sidewalk.
Because of you,
I learned to play on the safe side so I don't get hurt.
Because of you,
I find it hard to trust not only me, but ev'ryone
around me.
Because of you, I am afraid.

Bridge:
I watched you die,
I heard you cry ev'ry night in your sleep.
I was so young,
you should have known better than to lean on me.
You never thought of anyone else,
you just saw your pain.
And now I cry in the middle of the night
for the same damn thing.

Chorus:
Because of you,
I never stray too far from the sidewalk.
Because of you,
I learned to play on the safe side so I don't get hurt.
Because of you,
I try my hardest just to forget ev'rything.
Because of you,
I don't know how to let anyone else in.
Because of you,
I'm ashamed of my life because it's empty.
Because of you, I am afraid.
Because of you. Ah, because of you. Ooh, ooh.

Because of You

Words and Music by
KELLY CLARKSON, BEN MOODY
and DAVID HODGES

Slowly ♩ = 69

Intro

3 times

Ooh,_____ ooh,_____

ooh._____

Verse:

1. I will not make the same__ mis-takes__ that you_____ did. I_____
2. I lose my way, and it's not too long__ be-fore_____ you point it out.

will__ not let my-self cause my heart__ so much mis-er-y.
I can-not cry, be-cause I know__ that's weak-ness in__ your eyes.

I will not break__ the way__ you did,__ you fell__ so hard.
I'm forced to fake__ a smile,__ a laugh_____ ev-'ry day__ of my

I've learned the hard__ way_____ to
life. My heart can't pos-si-bly break when it

never let it get that far._____ Be - cause of
was-n't e - ven whole to start_____ with.

Chorus:

you, I nev-er stray__ too far from the side - walk. Be - cause of

you, I learned to play on the safe side so I don't_ get hurt._ Be - cause of

you, I find it hard to trust__ not on - ly me,__

__ but ev-'ry-one_ a - round_ me. Be - cause_ of you,_____ I am af - raid._

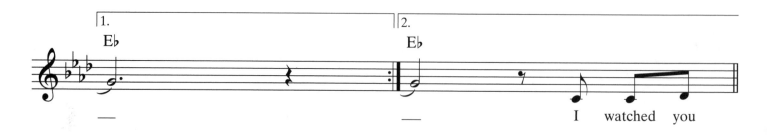

1.
_____

2.
_____ I watched you

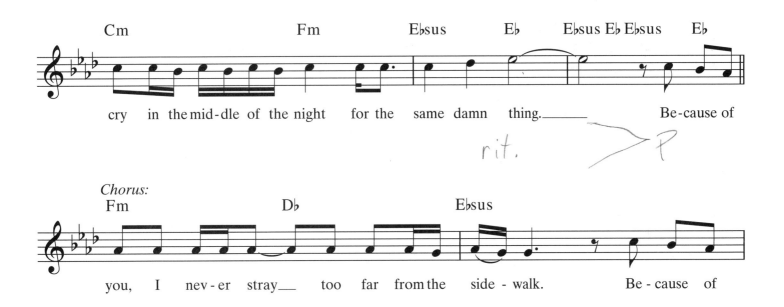

you, I try my hard-est just_ to for - get ev - 'ry - thing._ Be - cause of

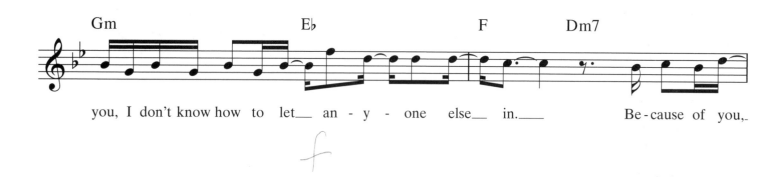

you, I don't know how to let_ an - y - one else_ in._ Be - cause of you,_

_ I'm a-shamed of my life_ be-cause it's emp - ty. Be-cause of you,_

_ I am af - raid._ Be - cause_ of you._ Ah,_____

_ be - cause_ of you._ Ooh,_____ ooh.__

Because You Loved Me

Words and Music by
DIANE WARREN

Verse 1:
For all those times you stood by me,
for all the truth that you made me see,
for all the joy you brought to my life,
for all the wrong that you made right,
for ev'ry dream you made come true,
for all the love I found in you,
I'll be forever thankful, baby.
You're the one who held me up,
never let me fall.
You're the one who saw me through,
through it all.

Chorus:
You were my strength when I was weak,
you were my voice when I couldn't speak.
You were my eyes when I couldn't see,
you saw the best there was in me,
lifted me up when I couldn't reach.
You gave me faith 'coz you believed.
I'm ev'rything I am because you loved me.

Verse 2:
You gave me wings and made me fly,
you touched my hand, I could touch the sky.
I lost my faith, you gave it back to me.
You said no star was out of reach,
you stood by me and I stood tall.
I had your love, I had it all.
I'm grateful for each day you gave me.
Maybe I don't know that much,
but I know this much is true.
I was blessed because I was loved by you.

Chorus:
You were my strength when I was weak,
you were my voice when I couldn't speak.
You were my eyes when I couldn't see,
you saw the best there was in me,
lifted me up when I couldn't reach.
You gave me faith 'coz you believed.
I'm ev'rything I am because you loved me.

Bridge:
Oh. You were always there for me,
the tender wind that carried me.
A light in the dark,
shining your love into my life.
You've been my inspiration,
through my lies, you were the truth.
My world is a better place because of you.

Chorus:
You were my strength when I was weak,
you were my voice when I couldn't speak.
You were my eyes when I couldn't see,
you saw the best there was in me,
lifted me up when I couldn't reach.
You gave me faith 'coz you believed.
I'm ev'rything I am because you loved me.
You were my strength when I was weak,
you were my voice when I couldn't speak.
You were my eyes when I couldn't see,
you saw the best there was in me,
lifted me up when I couldn't reach.
You gave me faith 'coz you believed.
I'm ev'rything I am because you loved me.
I'm ev'rything I am because you loved me.

Because You Loved Me

Words and Music by
DIANE WARREN

*A piano chord is provided at the beginning of the play-along recording as a pitch reference for the vocalist.

Because You Loved Me - 4 - 1
26487

Because You Loved Me - 4 - 2
26487

10

Because You Loved Me - 4 - 3
26487

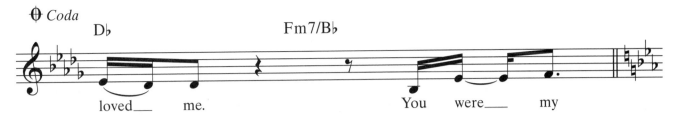

Coda
loved___ me. You were___ my

strength when I___ was weak, you were_ my voice when I could-n't speak. You were_ my

eyes when I could-n't see, you saw_ the best there was_ in me, lift - ed___ me___

up when I could-n't reach. You gave_ me faith 'coz you_ be - lieved.___ I'm

ev - 'ry - thing_ I am be - cause_ you loved_ me. I'm

ev - 'ry - thing_ I am_____ be - cause_ you loved_ me.___

Believe

Words and Music by
BRIAN HIGGINS, STUART McLENNAN, PAUL BARRY,
STEPHEN TORCH, MATT GRAY and TIM POWELL

Verse 1:
No matter how hard I try,
you keep pushing me aside
and I can't break through,
there's no talking to you.
It's so sad that you're leaving,
takes time to believe it.
But after all is said and done,
you're gonna be the lonely one, oh.

Chorus:
Do you believe in life after love?
I can feel something inside me say,
I really don't think you're strong enough, no.
Do you believe in life after love?
I can feel something inside me say,
I really don't think you're strong enough, no.

Verse 2:
What am I supposed to do,
sit around and wait for you?
Well, I can't do that,
and there's no turning back.
I need time to move on,
I need love to feel strong.
'Cause I've had time to think it through,
and maybe I'm too good for you, oh.

Chorus:
Do you believe in life after love?
I can feel something inside me say,
I really don't think you're strong enough, no.
Do you believe in life after love?
I can feel something inside me say,
I really don't think you're strong enough, no.

Bridge:
Well, I know that I'll get through this,
'cause I know that I am strong.
And I don't need you anymore,
I don't need you anymore.
I don't need you anymore,
no, I don't need you anymore.

Chorus:
Do you believe in life after love?
I can feel something inside me say,
I really don't think you're strong enough, no.
Do you believe in life after love?
I can feel something inside me say,
I really don't think you're strong enough, no.
Do you believe in life after love?
I can feel something inside me say,
I really don't think you're strong enough, no.
Do you believe in life after love?
I can feel something inside me say,
I really don't think you're strong enough, no.

Believe

Words and Music by
BRIAN HIGGINS, STUART McLENNAN, PAUL BARRY,
STEPHEN TORCH, MATT GRAY and TIM POWELL

Disco beat ♩ = 132

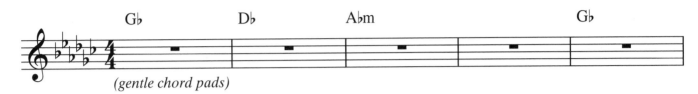

(gentle chord pads)

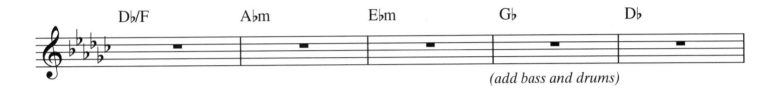

(add bass and drums)

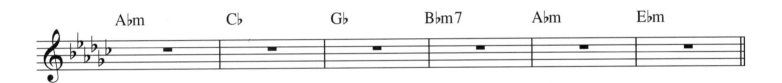

Verse:

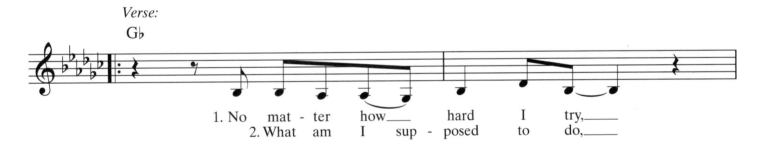

1. No mat-ter how____ hard I try,____
2. What am I sup-posed to do,____

you keep push-ing me a-side____ and I can't____
sit a-round and wait for you?____ Well, I can't____

____ break through,
____ do that,

there's no
and there's

14

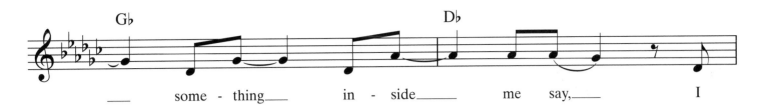

some - thing___ in - side___ me say,___ I

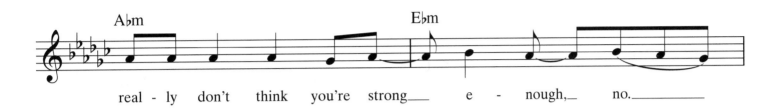

real - ly don't think you're strong___ e - nough,___ no.___

Do you be - lieve___ in life___ af - ter love?___

I can feel___ some - thing___ in - side___ me say,___ I

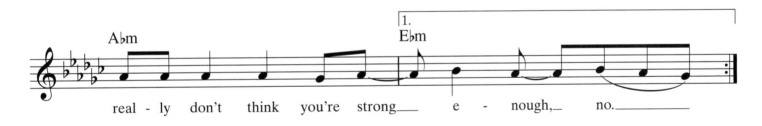

real - ly don't think you're strong___ e - nough,___ no.___

___ e - nough,___ no.___ Well, I know___

___ that I'll___ get through this,___

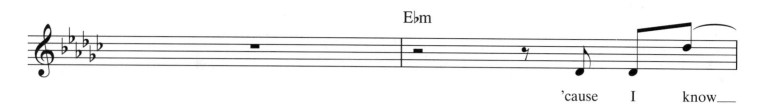

'cause I know___

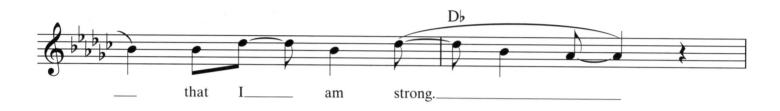

___ that I___ am strong.___

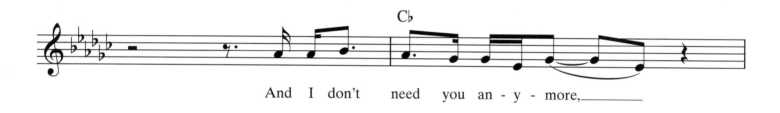

And I don't need you an - y - more,___

I don't need you an - y - more.___

I___ don't need___ you an - y - more,___

no, I don't need___ you an - y - more.___

Chorus:

Do you be - lieve___ in life___ af - ter love?___

I can feel___ some - thing___ in - side___ me say,___ I

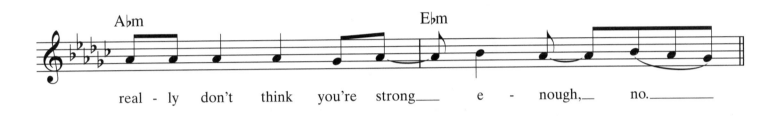

real - ly don't think you're strong___ e - nough,___ no.___

Do you be - lieve___ in life___ af - ter love?___

I can feel___ some - thing___ in - side___ me say,___ I

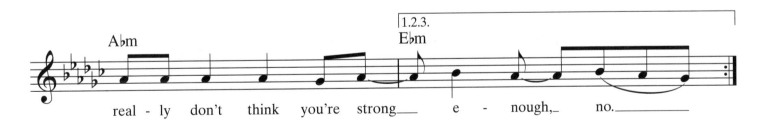

real - ly don't think you're strong___ e - nough,___ no.___

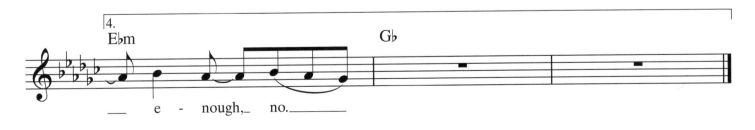

___ e - nough,___ no.___

Chain of Fools

Words and Music by
DON COVAY

Chorus:
Chain, chain, chain,
chain, chain, chain.
Chain, chain, chain,
chain of fools.

Verse 1:
For five long years
I thought you were my man.
But I found out, yeah,
I'm just a link in your chain, oh, yeah.
You got me where you want me,
I ain't nothin' but your fool.
You treated me mean,
oh, you treated me cruel.
Chain, chain, chain, chain of fools.

Verse 2:
Every chain
has got a weak link.
I might be weak, child,
but I feel the strain, oh, yeah.
You tell me to leave you alone.
My father said, "Come on home."
My doctor said, "Take it easy."
Oh, but your lovin' is much too strong.

Chorus:
I'm added to your chain, chain, chain,
chain, chain, chain.
Chain, chain, cha-a-a-a-ain,
chain of fools.

Verse 3:
One of these mornings
your chain is gonna break.
But up until then, yeah,
I'm gonna take all I can take, oh, yeah.

Chorus:
Chain, chain, chain,
chain, chain, chain.
Chain, chain, cha-a-a-a-ain,
chain of fools.
Chain, chain, chain,
chain, chain, chain.
Chain, chain, cha-a-a-a-ain,
chain of fools.
Oh, yeah.

Chain of Fools

Words and Music by
DON COVAY

Moderate R & B ♩ = 108

Chain, chain,_ chain,_

Chorus:

chain, chain, chain._____

Chain, chain,_ chain,_____ chain of fools._

Verse 1:

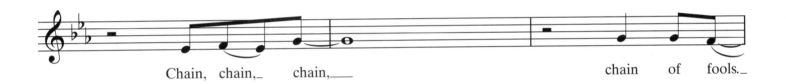

_____ 1. For five long_ years_____

I thought you were my man._____ But I found_

out,_____ yeah,_ I'm just a link in your chain,_ oh,_____

yeah. You got me where you want me, I ain't noth-in' but your fool.

You treat-ed me mean,— oh,

you treat-ed me cruel.— Chain, chain,— chain,—

Chorus:

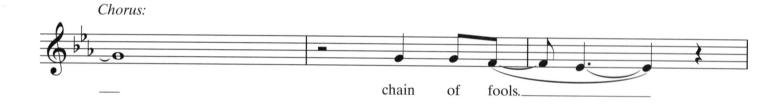

chain of fools.

Verse 2:

2. Ev-er-y chain— has got a weak—

link. I might be weak,— child,—

but I— feel— the strain,— oh,— yeah.—

You tell___ me to leave_ you a - lone.___ My fa -

ther said, "Come on___ home."___ My doc - tor said, "Take it eas-

y." Oh, but your lov-in' is___ much too___ strong._ I'm add-ed to your

Chorus:
Cm

chain, chain,___ chain,_____ chain, chain, chain._

_____ Chain, chain,_ cha - a - a - a -

ain, chain of fools._____ 3. One of these morn-

Verse 3:

ings your chain is gon - na break._

But up un-til then,_____ yeah,_____ I'm

gon-na take all I can take,___ oh,_____ yeah. Chain, chain,_ chain,_

Chorus:

chain, chain, chain._____

Chain, chain,_ cha - a - a - a - ain, chain of fools._

1. | 2.

_____ Chain, chain,_ chain,_ _____ Oh,_

Cm7   B♭ C7(♯9)

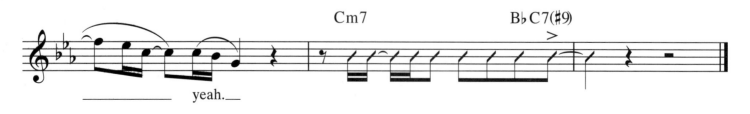

_____ yeah._

The Greatest Love of All

Words by LINDA CREED
Music by MICHAEL MASSER

Verse 1:
I believe the children are our future,
teach them well and let them lead the way.
Show them all the beauty they possess inside,
give them a sense of pride to make it easier.
Let the children's laughter
remind us how we used to be.

Verse 2:
Ev'rybody's searching for a hero,
people need someone to look up to.
I never found anyone who fulfilled my needs.
A lonely place to be, and so I
learned to depend on me.

I decided long ago
never to walk in anyone's shadow.
If I fail, if I succeed,
at least I lived as I believe.
No matter what they take from me,
they can't take away my dignity.

Chorus:
Because the greatest love of all
is happening to me.
I found the greatest love of all
inside of me.
The greatest love of all
is easy to achieve.
Learning to love yourself,
it is the greatest love of all.

Verse 3:
I believe the children are our future,
teach them well and let them lead the way.
Show them all the beauty they possess inside,
give them a sense of pride to make it easier.
Let the children's laughter
remind us how we used to be.

I decided long ago
never to walk in anyone's shadow.
If I fail, if I succeed,
at least I lived as I believe.
No matter what they take from me,
they can't take away my dignity.

Chorus:
Because the greatest love of all
is happening to me.
I found the greatest love of all
inside of me.
The greatest love of all
is easy to achieve.
Learning to love yourself,
it is the greatest love of all.
And if by chance that special place
that you've been dreaming of
leads you to a lonely place,
find your strength in love.

The Greatest Love of All

Words by LINDA CREED
Music by MICHAEL MASSER

Slowly ♩ = 72

Verses 1 & 2:

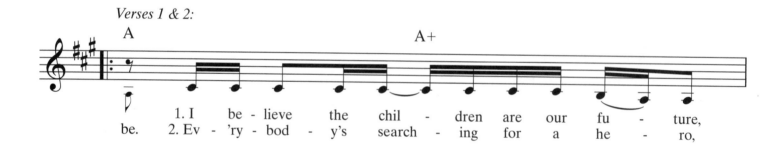

be. 1. I be - lieve the chil - dren are our fu - ture,
2. Ev - 'ry - bod - y's search - ing for a he - ro,

teach them well and let them lead the way.
peo - ple need some - one to look up to.

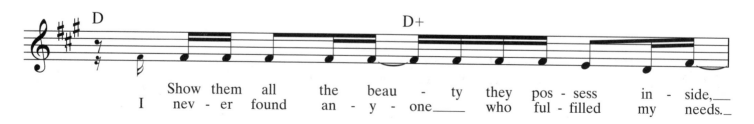

Show them all the beau - ty they pos - sess in - side,
I nev - er found an - y - one who ful - filled my needs.

The Greatest Love of All - 4 - 1
26487

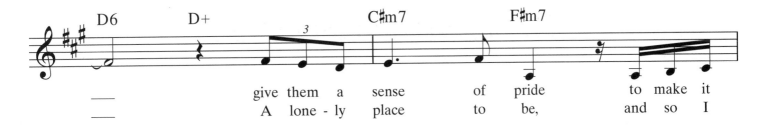

give them a sense of pride to make it

A lone-ly place to be, and so I

1.

eas - i - er.___ Let the chil-dren's laugh - ter___ re -

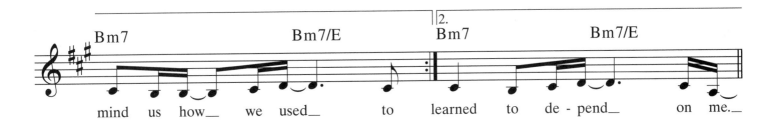

2.

mind us how___ we used___ to learned to de - pend___ on me.___

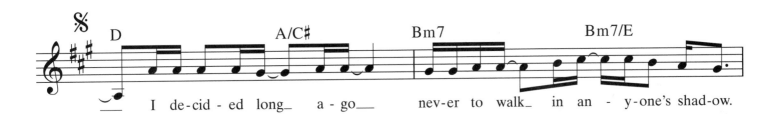

I de-cid - ed long___ a - go___ nev-er to walk___ in an - y-one's shad-ow.

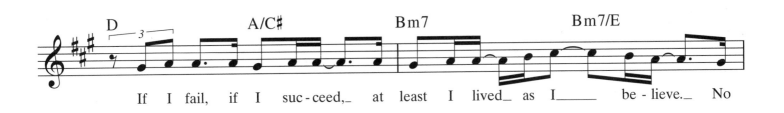

If I fail, if I suc-ceed,___ at least I lived___ as I_____ be - lieve.___ No

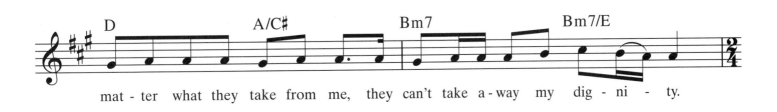

mat - ter what they take from me, they can't take a-way my dig - ni - ty.

The Greatest Love of All - 4 - 2
26487

26

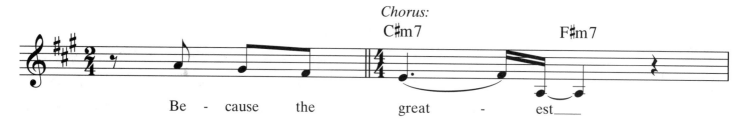
Chorus:
Be - cause the great - est___

love of all___ is hap - pen - ing___ to me.___

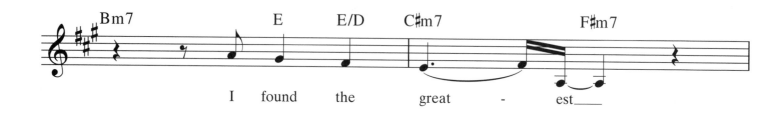
I found the great - est___

love of all___ in - side___ of me. The great - est___

love___ of all is eas - y to a - chieve.__

Learn - ing___ to love your - self,___ it is the

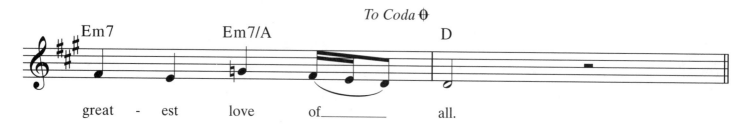
To Coda
great - est love of_____ all.

The Greatest Love of All - 4 - 3
26487

The Greatest Love of All - 4 - 4
26487

Hero

Words and Music by
WALTER AFANASIEFF and MARIAH CAREY

Verse 1:
There's a hero if you look inside your heart.
You don't have to be afraid of what you are.
There's an answer if you reach into your soul
and the sorrow that you know will melt away.

Chorus:
And then a hero comes along
with the strength to carry on
and you cast your fears aside
and you know you can survive.
So when you feel like hope is gone,
look inside you and be strong.
And you'll fin'lly see the truth,
that a hero lies in you.

Verse 2:
It's a long road when you face the world alone.
No one reaches out a hand for you to hold.
You can find love if you search within yourself
and the emptiness you felt will disappear.

Chorus:
And then a hero comes along
with the strength to carry on
and you cast your fears aside
and you know you can survive.
So when you feel like hope is gone,
look inside you and be strong.
And you'll fin'lly see the truth,
that a hero lies in you.

Bridge:
Lord knows, dreams are hard to follow,
but don't let anyone tear them away.
Hold on, there will be tomorrow.
In time you'll find the way.

Chorus:
And then a hero comes along
with the strength to carry on
and you cast your fears aside
and you know you can survive.
So when you feel like hope is gone,
look inside you and be strong.
And you'll fin'lly see the truth,
that a hero lies in you.
That a hero lies in you,
that a hero lies in you.

Hero

Words and Music by
WALTER AFANASIEFF
and MARIAH CAREY

Hero - 3 - 1
26487

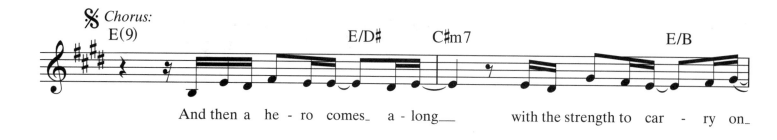

And then a he - ro comes_ a - long__ with the strength to car - ry on_

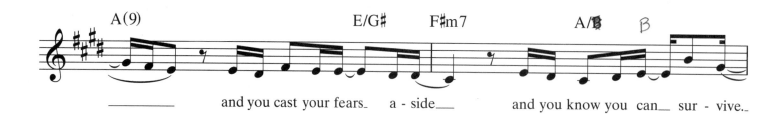

_____ and you cast your fears_ a - side__ and you know you can_ sur - vive._

_____ So when you feel like hope_ is gone,_ look in-side you and_ be strong._

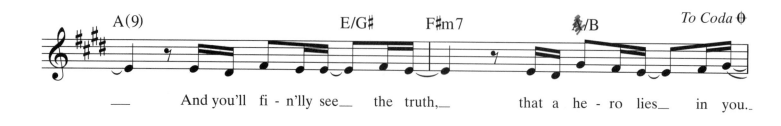

__ And you'll fi - n'lly see__ the truth,__ that a he - ro lies_ in you._

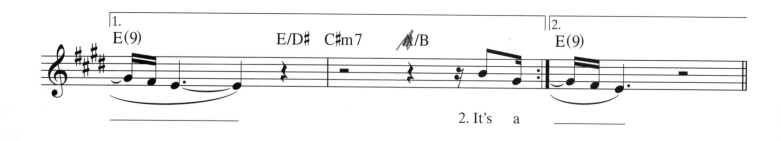

_____ 2. It's a _____

31

Lord___ knows,_____ dreams are hard_ to fol-low,

but don't let an-y-one tear them a-way.___

Hold___ on,_____ there will be_ to-mor-row.

In time you'll find the way.

That a he-ro lies in you,_____

that a he-ro lies in you.

Hero - 3 - 3
26487

How Do I Live

From the Touchstone Motion Picture *Con Air*
Words and Music by
DIANE WARREN

Verse 1:

How do I get through one night without you?
If I had to live without you, what kind of life would that be?
Oh, I, I need you in my arms, need you to hold.
You're my world, my heart, my soul.
And if you ever leave, baby, you would take away ev'rything good in my life.

Chorus:

And tell me now, how do I live without you? I want to know.
How do I breathe without you, if you ever go?
How do I ever, ever survive?
How do I, how do I, oh, how do I live?

Verse 2:

Without you, there'd be no sun in my sky,
there would be no love in my life, there'd be no world left for me.
And I, baby, I don't know what I would do,
I'd be lost if I lost you.
If you ever leave, baby, you would take away ev'rything real in my life.

Chorus:

And tell me now, how do I live without you? I want to know.
How do I breathe without you, if you ever go?
How do I ever, ever survive?
How do I, how do I, oh, how do I live?
Please tell me, baby, how do I go on?

Bridge:

If you ever leave, well, baby, you would take away ev'rything.
Need you with me.
Baby, don't you know that you're ev'rything good in my life?

Chorus:

And tell me now, how do I live without you? I want to know.
How do I breathe without you, if you ever go?
How do I ever, ever survive?
How do I, how do I, oh, how do I live?
How do I live without you?
How do I live?

How Do I Live

From the Touchstone Motion Picture *Con Air*

Words and Music by
DIANE WARREN

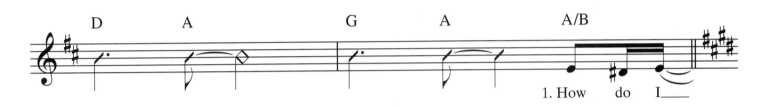

1. How do I___

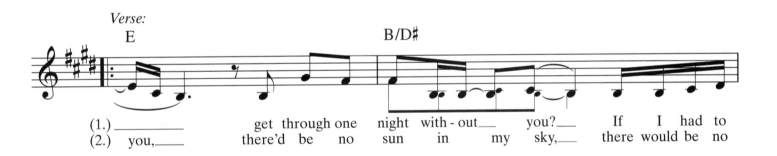

Verse:

(1.) ___ get through one night with-out___ you?___ If I had to
(2.) you,___ there'd be no sun in my sky,___ there would be no

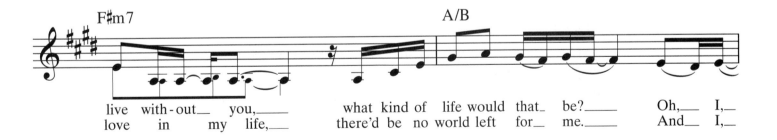

live with-out___ you,___ what kind of life would that___ be?___ Oh,___ I,___
love in my life,___ there'd be no world left for___ me.___ And___ I,___

___ I need you in my arms, need you___ to hold.___ You're my
___ ba - by, I don't know what I___ would do,___ I'd be

34

Take My Breath Away

By
GIORGIO MORODER and TOM WHITLOCK

Mmm, oh yeah.

Verse 1:
Watching ev'ry motion in
my foolish lover's game,
on this endless ocean,
fin'lly lovers know no shame.
Turning and returning
to some secret place inside,
watching in slow motion
as you turn around and say, my love,

Chorus:
"Take my breath away.
Take my breath away."

Verse 2:
Watching, I keep waiting,
still anticipating love.
Never hesitating,
to become the fated ones.
Turning and returning
to some secret place inside,
watching in slow motion
as you turn around and say, my love,

Chorus:
"Take my breath away.
Take my breath away."

Bridge:
Through the hourglass I saw you.
In time, you slipped away.
When the mirror crashed,
I called you and turned to hear you say,
"If only for today, I am unafraid."

Chorus:
Take my breath away.
You take my breath away.
You take my breath,
you take my breath,
you take my breath away.
You take my breath away,
you take my breath away,
you take my breath away.

Take My Breath Away

By
GIORGIO MORODER
and TOM WHITLOCK

Moderately ♩ = 100

Mmm,_____

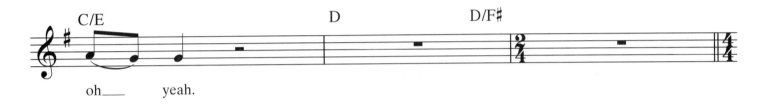

oh___   yeah.

Verse:

1. Watch-ing ev-'ry mo-tion in_____ my fool-ish lov-er's game,_____
2. Watch-ing, I keep wait-ing, still_____ an - tic - i - pat - ing love._____

on this end-less o-cean, fi — n'lly lov-ers know   no shame._
Nev-er hes-i-tat-ing, to_____   be-come the   fat-ed

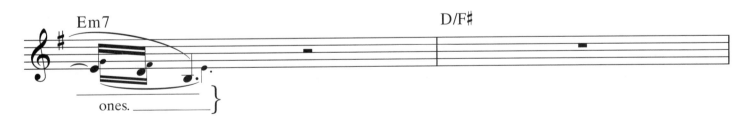

ones. _____

Turn-ing and re-turn-ing to_____ some se-cret place in-side,_____

38

watch-ing in slow mo - tion as____ you turn a-round and say,__

____ my love, "Take my breath a -

Chorus:

way._____

Take my breath a - way."_____

1.   2.

Bridge:

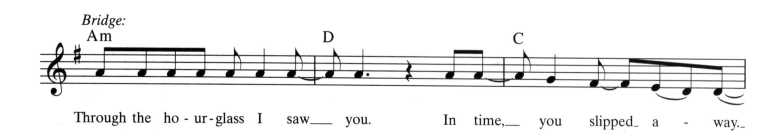

Through the ho - ur-glass I saw__ you.   In time,__ you slipped_ a - way.__

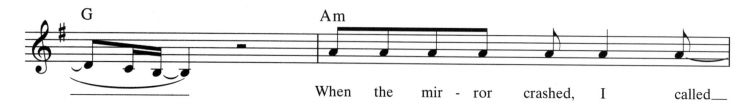

____ When the mir - ror crashed, I called__

Take My Breath Away - 3 - 2
26487

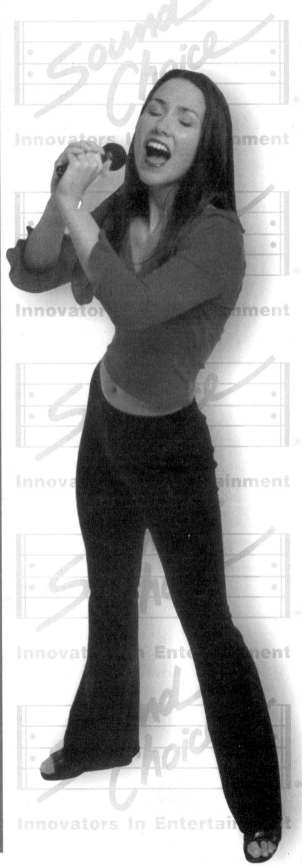